interior
desecrations

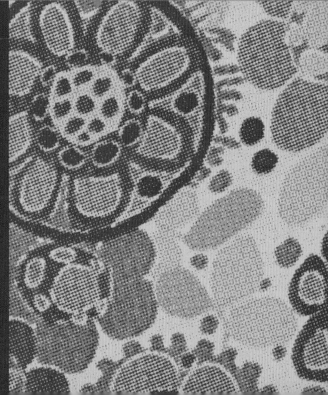

interior

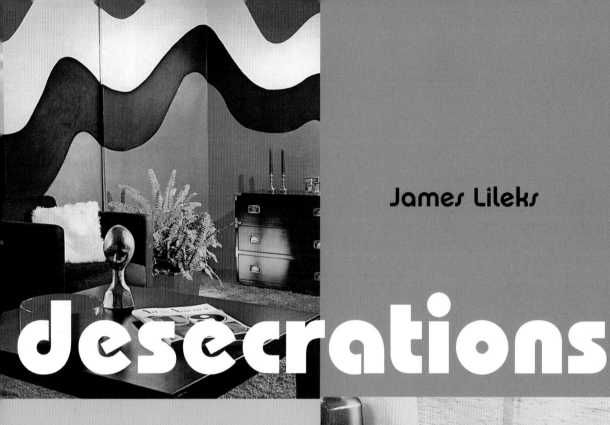

James Lileks

desecrations

Hideous Homes from the Horrible '70s

Three Rivers Press, New York

also by james lileks

The Gallery of Regrettable Food

Fresh Lies

Notes of a Nervous Man

Mr. Obvious

Falling Up the Stairs

Published by Three Rivers Press, an imprint of
the Crown Publishing Group, a division of Random House, Inc., New York.
www.crownpublishing.com

Originally published in hardcover in the United States by Crown Publishers, a division of Random
House, Inc., New York, in 2004.

THREE RIVERS PRESS and the Tugboat colophon are registered trademarks
of Random House, Inc.

Library of Congress Cataloging-in-Publication Data
Lileks, James.
    Interior desecrations: hideous homes from the horrible '70s / by James Lileks.—1st ed.
    1. Interior decoration—United States—History—20th century.   2. Nineteen seventies—Humor.
3. Aesthetics, American.   I. Title.
NK2004.L55   2004
747'.0973'09047—dc22   2003070042

ISBN 0-307-23872-5

Printed in China

Design by Kay Schuckhart/Blond on Pond

10   9   8   7   6   5   4   3   2   1

First Paperback Edition

To George and Nancy, thrift-store scouts extraordinaire, and to all the patrons of lileks.com who asked—nay, demanded!—that a humble website about hideous wallpaper be turned into this book. Thanks!

Contents

warning: You must be this dorky to read this book.

introduction

THIS IS A LABOR OF HATE.

It's a hate that burns like your knees burn after you've slid a yard on a harsh synthetic rug. A hate I've nourished and stoked for decades. I came of age in the '70s, and there were few crueler things you could inflict on a person. The music: either sluggish metal, cracker-boogie, or wimpy balladeers trying to cry their way into some granola-fed dropout's granny dress. Television: camp without the pleasure of knowing it's camp. The politics: the sweaty perfidy of Nixon, the damp uselessness of Ford, the sanctimonious impotence of Carter. The world: nasty. Hair: unspeakable. Architecture: metal-shingled mansard roofs on franchise chicken shops. No oil. No fun. Syphilis and Fonzie.

Of course, I exaggerate. At the time, everything seemed normal. Sure, things were a little . . . brown, a tad more orange than they'd been before. Yes, we knew our clothes were ridiculous when we wore them, but we all knew this wouldn't last. We'd all be nuked into a big long smear of red jam or dumped into a dystopian *Soylent Green* world, eating pressed wafers made of grandparents and kelp. Crank up the Foghat and get out the ZigZags, boys; let's live it up while we can. The '70s ended in 1977 with the Sex Pistols and New Wave; when college kids started wearing skinny ties and thrift-store Rat Pack jackets, they shot the '70s dead. The corpse remained standing and chatting for a few more years, but the battle was won. If you think the '80s were dumber than the '70s, either you weren't there or you weren't paying attention.

So what does this have to do with furniture?

Nothing. Everything. First, I want everyone who thinks the '70s were *hip!* to realize that this decade was the absolute opposite of hip. It was a breathtakingly ugly period. Even the rats parted their hair down the middle. But most important: we must learn. This is what happens when an entire culture becomes so besotted by the New, the Hip, the With-It Styles that they can't object to orange plaid wallpaper—because they fear they'll look square.

This is what happens when Dad drinks, Mom floats in a Valium haze, the kids slump down to the den with the bong, and the decorator has such a desperate coke habit he simply *must* convince half the town to put up reflective wallpaper or he's going to lose his kneecaps to his supplier's enforcer. Just say no? They couldn't. They didn't know why they should.

No, I am not saying *your* mom was hopped up on goofballs. But all it takes is a few trendsetters who fall for this stuff and set the styles for the rest

COPY EDITORS who handled this book were observed jabbing pencils into their eyes after seven or more pages.

TO PREVENT willful self-blinding, we ask you to perform a few adjustments that will recalibrate your sense of aesthetics.

THE AUTHOR and the publisher are not responsible for the consequences of viewing these pictures without adequate preparation.

PLEASE READJUST your sense of taste, appreciation, and love of all that is holy and decent until you can view this image without barfing up lunch into your lap.

of Middle America. Soon the rest of the nation finds out it has no choice—it's rotten-avocado-colored fabrics and shiny-foil wallpaper or nothing.

So where did these horrors come from? You guess:

1. They were part of a Soviet psychological torture program used to make dissident decorators crack and confess. "Look at it, comrade—look at the decadent ugliness of the West! All that money, and they still mix checks and plaids! And you would betray honest Socialist fabrics for this? Confess!"

2. These illustrations were conceived in the mid-'50s as a benchmark—if a critical mass of middle-class homes started to look this bad, the government would realize there had been a catastrophic failure of national taste, the sort of thing that demoralizes an entire generation and leads to draft riots and Bolshevism. The Feds would declare Martial Law for Interior Design. The National Guard would step in, strip the walls, and paint everything white. This never actually happened, because Betty Ford countermanded the Executive Order. She *liked* the eel-green fleur-de-lis pattern on the wallpaper, the sofa, the rug, and the curtains. Men! What did they know?

3. It's just dubious advice from the usual suspects: common magazines from the grocery store, books put out by Trusted Names in domestic guidance, and other sources whose archives are curiously missing several years, as if

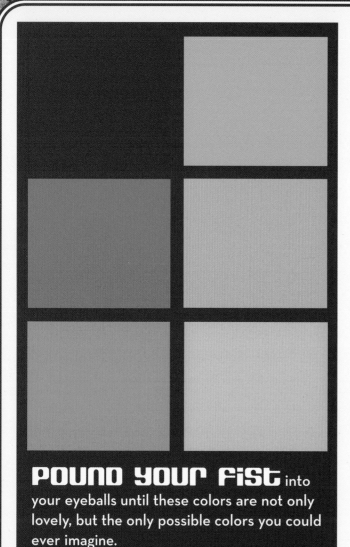

POUND YOUR FIST into your eyeballs until these colors are not only lovely, but the only possible colors you could ever imagine.

they're ashamed of the advice they once gave. "Lost the pictures in the fire," they'll tell you. "That fire we had, uh, during the earthquake, uh, after the comet hit, and . . ." Then they hang up.

We need to face this stuff. We need to accept the otherwise sensible American wives who would never grind up a quaalude into their Metrecal or sleep with their tennis instructor nevertheless went daft at some point. They ripped out these pages, thrust them under the nose of their designer, and said, "I want this right here,

stare at this image until the bed and the rug actually start to look as if they belong in the same galaxy. This may take a while. Do not mistake hunger-induced delirium for aesthetic enjoyment.

DOES THIS

cushion pattern resemble:

1. The hide of a fly's arse, plucked of its hair and horribly magnified?

2. Used cigarette filters from the planet Hexagonia?

3. That pattern you were just thinking of using in the living room for the drapes (and we can make matching jumpsuits for the entire family out of the leftover scraps!)?

If 3, you're ready. Let's begin.

exactly, only a little less Annie Hall and a little more *Kramer vs. Kramer* in the entryway, okay? Not so much the white shag everywhere—we have kids—but I am really into these plastic pillows here, okay? And I want a big letter nailed to the wall like Rhoda had on her show."

And the designer thinks: *It was Mary Tyler Moore who had the letter on the wall, you idiot, but that's okay. That's just fine. In seven years we're going to begin Project Laura Ashley, and you're going to drain hubby dry for that one. By the time the magazines are done with you, you'll be begging for chintz drapes on your rearview mirror.*

"Rhoda it is!" he says.

No, we need to face this now. Here's the argument in the case of Taste vs. the Seventies. Welcome to Hell: where it's always '73 and Sonny.

entryways

You'd have to take care leaving the house through these spaces; the sudden change in taste could give you the bends.

Look. Folks. It's simple. If you have poor taste in decorating, don't go nuts in the entryway. Wait until your guests are inside before you spring something unusual on them. *But,* you say, *doesn't that fabulous statuary look so* right *over by the door? It's an ancient Belgian God of Fertility or something. You can hang hats on the erection. Or use it for umbrellas!* That's not the point. Most people don't want to encounter this sort of thing right away, if ever. Especially one that's been handpainted in such a *unique* fashion. Put it in the spare bedroom; it'll keep houseguests from lingering.

One more rule for bad entryways: don't forget a small table with a bowl on top. It serves no use; there's nothing in the drawer; people bump into it when taking off their coats. But there must be a small table with a bowl on top. It's not the law, but it might as well be.

THE VISUAL

equivalent of granulated glass in your eyes. Looking hurts. Blinking hurts. Rubbing hurts. Blindness, when it comes, is almost a comfort.

It's one of those rooms that almost feels ashamed of itself:

Don't blame me. I had nothing to do with this. I couldn't move. I watched what they did to the kitchen, heard the cupboards scream out as they applied the dots, one by one by one. . . . I knew I was next and there was nothing I could do. It was horrible.

Atrocities like this are partly responsible for the founding, in 1977, of People for the Ethical Treatment of Entryways.

THIS IS A FOYER. This is the first impression. This is how you warn people your taste tends toward *interesting* colors, such as those found on the buttocks of a rudely shaved monkey.

says the note in the designer's guide that coughed up this picture: "Gigantic patterned wallpaper in a small area is exciting because it breaks all the rules." Well, a flaming pile of pig crap in the foyer breaks all the rules. Smearing goat brains on the walls breaks all the rules. Sometimes rules are there for a reason—such as keeping you from doing this.

"You can be adventurous in little-used areas." You mean little-used areas like the front door? What, did people enter through the chimney and leave through the coal chute?

FIGHTING CENTIPEDES?

A close-up of one's intestinal lining? Difficult to say. But you can be sure the designer chose this scheme because it "drew the eye upward." Of course, one could say the same thing about the *Hindenburg* disaster.

living rooms

The name for these parlors—*living room*—wasn't entirely inaccurate. Something *did* live there—a fern, perhaps. Some dust mites. A spider. But humans? Rarely. These were showplace rooms, mausoleums where the examples of domestic style were interred. On any given day the sofa and chairs would be sheathed with plastic condoms, lest the fabric be soiled; the drapes drawn lest the hard mean sun suck the color from the cushions. All these rooms needed to complete the picture was Lenin in a glass casket. The people who stuffed their living rooms with this horrid junk would probably have bought plastic covers for the plastic covers, if such a thing had been marketed. Think about it: Your plastic covers keep the fabrics fresh and clean, but what of the covers themselves? Dust, sunlight, pet dander, parakeet psoriasis—why, your plastic covers are depositories of domestic filth. Your friends understand why you keep the covers on when they drop by for a chat; you're saving the sofa for Company. But don't you owe it to friends to give them a surface that's Company fresh? Introducing new Cover Covers, from Dow Corning! No messy polyurethane rolls with DNA-mutating aromas; Cover Covers, which come in a handy spray can, keep covers fresh for centuries to come.

Or you could just rope off the room.

Or you could brick it up and show people pictures.

Laminate the pictures first. You can wipe off the fingerprints.

IF YOUR

social circle smokes so much you have to put out five ashtrays that look like dog-food bowls for robot St. Bernards, maybe white is not the right color for your sofa. Try something in a ground-in ash.

Science has been unable to determine the use or nature of this object, other than to signal the inability of the client to say no to her decorator. It is speculated that objects like this were left as messages to future decorators, telling them they can get away with *anything*.

Perhaps there's

such a thing as "room karma." If something horrible has happened in a space, the room must suffer along with those who perpetrated the evil. It will come back first as an ugly mess, then purify itself with incrementally better redecorations over the course of time.

This would be the first reincarnation, then. What happened here to deserve this monstrous design one can only guess; surely it started with someone in a clown suit sawing puppies in half, and just got worse.

And what's that on the coffee table? Ah, an egg on a pedestal. A clever interplay of organic shapes and man-made materials. A tripartite structure that recalls the columns of the Doric order, or the very human frame itself.

Also, a total piece of crap.

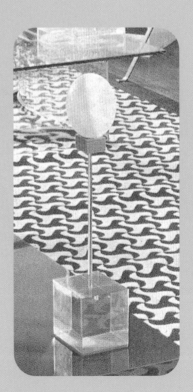

ANOTHER PROP from 2001.

Don't bring the monkeys into this room! They'll just start banging bones on the furniture when they see this black monolith.

Maybe it's a letter slot in a building where tenants like to rip off the drywall and mail it to people.

There's only one possible reaction to this artwork: *Gesundheit!*

WHY NOT lacquer all your Pekingese's boulevard bon-bons and string them on a line? This way you can remember little Lucy after she's gone, and it makes a cheap window treatment. Never mind the smell—after thirty years of Lucky Strikes, the last thing you smelled was when that tanker full of bleach overturned up the street.

SOMETIMES, just to amuse himself, Marvin would wear a shirt and slacks in the identical pattern as the floor. Camouflage, he called it. Useful for a mission behind enemy lines—which, in this case, was any room in which his wife was drawing breath. He would lie motionless for hours, listening to her gossip on the phone with the porridge-brained imbeciles in her social circle, hearing the *clinkety-clink* of the ice cubes as she drank off half her cocktail. Odd how she slurred most of her words by noon, but always pronounced "Gucci" with a nice crisp diction no matter what time of day it was. It was her form of devoutness, he decided.

He also enjoyed putting on the suit that matched the chair and sitting in silence while she sat across from him, working on her third vodka tonic of the evening. One of these nights he'd move, slightly. Stop her sodden heart for good, it should.

Let's buy this art book, she said. *It matches the walls.* Good God. Because it matched the walls. And the way she said the artist's name: Peh-CASS-o.

No jury in the land would convict him. At least not one with any taste.

For many years,

decorators seemed to believe that a lot of bad art somehow adds up to one piece of good art, the way quarters add up to dollars.

The largest and most incomprehensible item has been placed over the small fireplace, which makes the latter look like a tradesman's entrance for trolls, or an elevator for the house pets.

For extra fun, put a mirror on the wall that looks like an actual doorway, then amuse yourself at parties as people walk into it headfirst and spill their red wine down their shirt front.

Way up high is this oddity, which seems to show the Quaker Oats man amusing himself with one of those novelty invisible-dog leashes.

YOU JUST KNOW there's a De Lorean in the garage.
And a pound of blow in the closet.

No idea what this is. It appears to be a medium-size
dog coughing up a smaller one.

IT'S THE LATEST THING: indoor shag-lined wading pools. (When drained for cleaning, they make excellent conversation pits as well.)

AND NOW,

the winner of the Cram 'Er Full of Crap Competition, blue division. Hail the silver can! Hail the albino-dinosaur-prostate hanging lamp! Marvel at the audacious table placement—you'd have to be winched into place to fit between table and sofa.

But best of all—the touch that really, really makes the room: *Art nailed to the fireplace tiles*—with utter disregard for the ancient art of Spacing. Bravo!

A round of applause for the table art, which appears to be scavenged from a fire in a duck decoy factory.

SHINY CANS: check. Art based on the premise that you may have to do some bullfighting in the living room and will need a large red cape: check! Butt-cracking sofa that looks like a shop-class project: check! Rug woven from the sweepings of a hairstylist's salon the day *Vogue* declared highlights to be "out": check! Plastic tables you'll knock over the moment you stand up: check, and check! Meaningless, undustable artwork made entirely of empty drugstore cologne bottles: check! You're all set for the '70s! Have fun!

IF YOU had a persistent rash, this would be a good room; you'd look right at home. If you wanted a decor to blend in with the exploded capillaries on your alcoholic schnoz, this would be a good room. If you wanted a decor that contained so much red and so many candles that you could blame the sudden appearance of Satan on your furniture—"Well, I certainly wasn't *planning* to have orgiastic relations with the cloven-hoofed embodiment of evil and fear, but when he's standing there in the fireplace shouting, *You have summoned me!*, what is one to do?"—then this a good room.

Note: This is not a good room.

OH, everyone's doing living, mossy walls this year. Easy to care for—just hose them down weekly. Bring a little bit of the outdoors into your home! And of course that includes the sight of several thousand writhing grubworms and millipedes when you remove the painting to clean the glass.

Warn the servants. And keep the dogs off the sofa; they'll pull a haunch muscle trying to mark their territory.

NOTHING SAYS

Saturday morning like this Sid & Marty Krofft-inspired Huffawhumapsofalus. It comes predrenched in milk, and we've already stuffed a bushel of Trix, Count Chocula, Quisp, and Boo Berry down the cushion cracks. Comes with special Slidz-A-Part cushions that fall on the floor when you lean against them, and a thin little rolled back part that's too soft to use as a headrest, and too small to use as a backrest. So lean against the window! Fall through the glass? Cut yourself! Scream for Mom! Nothing says Saturday morning like a trip to the emergency room! You'll get a sucker!

For fun, stick starched Bozo hair in a used paint roller! Is this stuff safe, or full of chemicals known to cause reproductive disorders in lab mice? Probably the latter. But no one ever thinks to blame poor health on their bric-a-brac. Unless it's one of those Asbestos Misters from the '50s.

Don't forget the annoyingly meaningless art: it's the offspring of Ms. Pac-Man and the biohazard symbol.

HeRe we have a mix of old green crap, new green crap, and some stunning green transitional crap, all of which serve to give this room the exhausted, mealy flavor of overcooked vegetables. The owner has picked the most unattractive variety of cacti available—the ones that look like prickly billy clubs or particularly masochistic sex toys—and placed them by the fire, where they are certain to ignite, setting the rest of the house on fire within minutes.

To tie it all together, an oversize Chuck Close painting of a broccoli's MRI hangs over the fireplace. Why? Because that damn vegetable's relatives might come around looking for vengeance, and that's the first thing you want them to see: their kin, sliced in half, lightly steamed and nailed to the wall.

Let's see the CIA get their mind-control rays through this room! I was up all night carefully crushing beer cans to glue on the wall—and you have to use *only* Heinekens! The American cans have an ingredient in the aluminum that lets the rays right through—the government *made* them put it in—it's why the beer tastes funny—everyone knows it tastes funny but no one asks why—that's the rays at work—but you need to wear these pie plates in your pants too—don't ask—they'll hear—they have dogs downstairs trained to listen to everything I say—at night they say it back to their controllers in dog language which I have learned to decode, and it's frustrating when the dogs quote me wrong and I can't go correct them without giving myself away.

FOR THE slightly less insane who are slightly less afraid of CIA mind-control beams, wood will do. Keeps out most of the annoying orders. You get the occasional command (*"Must* gnaw neighbor's fences with front teeth and build dam in the backyard! *Must!"*), but if you readjust your paper hat, they go away.

IF YOU LIVED HERE, you'd be laid by now. If it was 1973, anyway. It's the lair of the Tasteful Swinging Batch—the mezzanine lined with unread books, the guitar to indicate your sensitive troubadour side, the TEAC reel-to-reel to show off your collection of progressive jazz, the TV sized just right for watching *Kojak* while you blow a number of primo Colombian (hey, Kojak may be the Man, but he's solid cool). There's even a recessed ladder in case you're upstairs and your date catches on fire or something and you have to get down quick.

He lost the house in the divorce in '79. Oh, she said it was because of his quaalude "problem," but she'd been planning this *way* before he ever took some Vitamin Q.

What do you mean, paranoid? Now you're sounding like *her*.

FOR THE Bond Supervillain on a budget.

It has a ledge, so your minions can topple off when shot. It has a ladder down which you can escape. It has fussy furniture whose old-world charms contrast with your Nehru-jacketed sense of icy-cool nihilism. It's not the sort of lair you'd be proud to show 007. But one of the lesser double-oughts? 002? 003? They'd hardly notice that the paintings are actually lithographs. And for that alone they deserve to die!

BY THE shores of Kitcheegoome
Crap was sold to matron lady
Who felt kinship with the Injun
And felt sad for extinct Bison
But her husband made fun of her
Come here, Squaw! he'd say! Why that cur
Mocked her sense of social justice
When the guests came he would insist
On a greeting that poked fun of
Native rhythms that she so loved:
"Hiya-Marge-and-Pete-and-Nancy!
Hiya-say-you're-looking-fancy!"

Out of vogue this style will soon be!
In then will be lamps Tiffany!
Sell this crap at loss she soon will.
Yell the husband will when he sees bill.

IN THE EARLY '70S, the nation was afflicted with incurable pattern viruses—small microbes that reproduced and multiplied from a single swatch left on a sofa, and soon covered the entire room. As we see here, it's infected the sofa, the walls, and the curtains; by the time it reached this point it had begun to affect crockery, cuticles, periodicals, and house pets as well.

When the dog's underbelly breaks out in repeated vases, the only thing you can do is burn down the house and quarantine the neighborhood.

THiS rOOM was designed for a blind blues singer, so he could hear the various pieces of furniture.

Over the sofa, it's Francis Bacon's *Skinned Horse Descending a Staircase.*

THERE is no God.

IF THERE is a God, what did we do to deserve *this*? At least the entire room isn't ruined by this pattern—as the mirror shows, the other wall is ruined by an entirely different pattern. Perhaps this is God's punishment for insufficient devotion:

"And a third part of their dwellings shall be wrapped in fabric, and the whole of their sofas shall suffer likewise, and the fourth part of their walls sheathed in a style whose contrasting nature is loud and vexatious like the clashing of shields, and this shall make them rent their suits of leisure and wail: 'O, how wicked are we that we must dwell in this place the rest of our days?'"

Pretty damned wicked, apparently.

OKAY, maybe there *is* a God, but he's just not a hands-on kind of guy. He gives us free will. We can do with it as we please, with the knowledge that we will answer for our lives—and our choice of rugs—in the next world.

It is said that dogs cannot see color, only muted shades of gray. It is also said that dogs do not go to heaven.

Given this room, it seems a fair deal.

TO UNDERSTAND the full visual horror of this era, you have to visualize a man in plaid pants sitting on the sofa. Or any patterned pants, for that matter: this was a sofa designed to clash with humans. Nude people would clash with this sofa. Albino nude people would clash with this sofa. The Invisible Man would clash with this sofa. It is one of those perfectly rare pieces of furniture that clashes with itself. Just looking at it makes you feel as if you've bounced down the stairs in a box of cymbals. It would accept gigantic chameleons who had spent a year in an oddly colored circus tent, but no humans.

The art is typical up-with-people beauty from this era: charred lumber stuck to a board, framed, and hung.

THE ONLY possible explanation: the sofa was bolted to the floor and wired to a bomb that would kill anyone if they tried to remove it. No other reason why this thing would be here in this picture. One can accept the curtains and the rug; they're related, although "related" in the sense of hillbilly siblings who marry and breed. The ornate baroque mirror could be seen as an ironic counterpoint to the spindly mod Lucite table, if one is feeling generous. One of the chairs can claim the blue excuse for being here, the other one has the most tenuous connection of them all—it's as green as the alien sofa, and its wickerlicious style has no allies in the room.

It's possible this is a spare room where the design team kept furniture for real layouts, and a picture of it was mistaken for an actual design.

Out of the picture on the left is a light fixture so bright it casts shadows of the other lamps, making one wonder why you'd *need* another lamp. Particularly since the room itself glows like a Chernobyl technician's thyroid.

FRIENDS don't let friends paint and drink.

bathrooms

Modern rooms for modern bowels.

The destruction of the dual-hued tiled bathroom is one of the great aesthetic crimes of the '70s. Granted, all that tile gave the room an acoustic signature that amplified any reports one might make in the room—given enough beans, one could stir the curtains. But the lurid, hip, with-it! bathrooms that replaced the tiled rooms of yore seemed less like bathrooms than bright cloakrooms with unexpected amounts of plumbing. What they gained in "style" they lost in soul. They weren't honest places anymore. They seemed ashamed of their purpose. Decorative soap and ceremonial towels meant one thing: you had to spit on your hands and dry them on the back pockets of your brown corduroy pants.

THiS iS the room equivalent of those guest towels no one feels comfortable using. No guest would dare to have a movement here. And if you did, it had better be small, compact, noiseless, free of aroma, and preferably ceramic, making a bell-like *clink!* as it hits the bottom of the bowl. Remember! *Excrete* rhymes with *discreet.*

This is Drapius, Patron-Saint of Unemployed Curtain Rod Salesmen.

WELL, it's nice to see they got some use out of those sets from *2001: A Space Odyssey*. You almost expect one of the astronauts to blow in and bounce around the room.

But who would buy it? Why, the fellow who struck it rich in the late '70s as a fern dealer (sell the ferns to restaurants at a discount, and make your money on the twice-weekly watering contracts). His therapist said he liked it because it gave him the birth-canal experience he had been denied as a C-section baby.

Prior to that revelation, he thought he liked it because it was just bitchin' wicked.

It has *stereo toilets!*

What happened to these cushions? They belonged nowhere else. No other decade so relished these tampons-of-the-gods; where did they go? Well, the people who bought this house from the original owner redid the room—did it all in a Mexican theme, actually—and the pillows went to the storage space in the basement until '81, when Junior at college took them for his first "pad." He gave them to a roommate who left school, moved to another place, and skipped out on his lease; the landlord gave them to the Salvation Army, who gave them to a homeless shelter.

Currently they exist in greatly diminished form in a tunnel adjacent to the A train line in Manhattan.

IT'S THE Junior Pothead Confuse-O-Room, specially designed to Like, Mess with Your Mind Totally. I mean, what if there isn't really a mirror there at all, and there's like a duplicate room on the other side? And what if Mom and Dad had like, plastic surgery performed on this guy to look like me, and that's him in the glass, and he reports back to them about all the stuff he sees me do in here? The only way to make sure is to break the window, but then they'd know I'm stoned.

Hey, how long have I been in here? It's been hours! They'll know I'm stoned just by how long I've been in here! And I left everything out on the table!

Wait a minute, this is Jason's house, not mine.

So what's this guy doing in the mirror at his house? It should be Jason's double on the other side! We caught them! They made a mistake! I've got to go tell him! This is incredible!

(Two hours later, slumped in front of the twenty-one-inch Magnavox, watching Saturday Night Live, which is great, because those guys are so high.)

"Uh, your bathroom—it's, uh, like—"

"It's over there, man."

"Uh—right."

This is America, right here: the host puts out a towel, but no one will use it, because it's so nicely folded. So the host puts out another, more casually folded towel on top of the towel for guests to use. But still the guest freezes: the way the black plays off the red, the way the disorder of the former contrasts with the precision of the latter—*I dare not disturb this ingenious tableau. I must wipe my hands on my pants. There is no way out.*

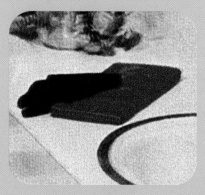

THE UBIQUITOUS and helpful arrow directs us to the location of the towel rack, which otherwise would have utterly escaped our detection. Presumably there is a gigantic DOWN arrow over the toilet as well, and perhaps a siren over the toilet-paper roll that goes off every six minutes in case you forget where the Charmin is.

Whoever painted the tub and feet—and we can safely assume it was a single twenty-something female in lower Manhattan who described herself in her *New York* personal as "half Grace Slick, half Annie Hall"—was cursed to hell twenty years later by the single forty-something female who bought this place as a co-op and spent nine consecutive Saturdays getting the goddamn paint off.

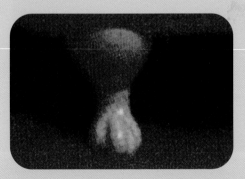

We can't really blame the '70s for this, but: What's the deal with putting animal feet on tubs? It's like insisting that all pianos should have tails, or dinner tables should have scrotal sacs. One of the things we like about tubs is their immobility, their general disinclination to bolt out of the room, scramble down the stairs, and make for the woods in a blind feral panic.

bedrooms

It's inexplicable, really.

Bedrooms are for sleeping. They are places of rest and composure. Chambers of peace. So why design them in styles that are the visual equivalent of someone taking a cheese grater to your gums? You *cannot sleep* in some of the rooms that follow, because the wallpaper's too loud. You cannot slip into REM sleep because the rug has a plaid that clashes like a bag full of trash-can lids tossed into a cement mixer. Even if you could tune out the living room, drink yourself into the sort of stupor that blotted out the horrors of the bathroom, you'd still be jabbed awake at 3 A.M. on some deep psychic level: "Helllllloooo. It's the draperies speaking. We're dyed the same bright red you'd expect to see if you slit the throat of a set designer for *Laugh-In*. We're watching youuuu. Aaaalllways watching."

This was also the golden age of One Pattern Fits All, as you'll see. Sheets, comforters, wallpaper, curtains, pillows, chairs—everything had one pattern. You could wear a suit in that pattern and be completely invisible.

Very popular with the Witness Protection set.

once upon a time these magnificent beasts roamed the land in herbs that seemed to stretch to the horizon.

Years of slaughter for their prized pelts have reduced them to a mere handful, and they are currently a protected species. This is one of the last remaining pairs.

Attempts to mate them in captivity have been unsuccessful. For which one can only give thanks.

Watch Your Step —we had an oil spill here this morning.

No question why the tenant painted the floor shiny black; helps you locate those stray atoms of cocaine you'll be looking for twelve hours after you had that runaway heartbeat and flushed the stash down the toilet. You can understand painting the doors, walls, and ceiling black, because—well, no, you really can't understand that. Maybe they were having a sale on black paint. Maybe it was the style of the moment. Maybe the landlord couldn't get the blood off the walls no matter how hard he scrubbed, and figured that if he painted the place no one would call it the Manson Practice Chamber anymore.

What really stumps us is the thing that hangs over the bed. Surely something this awful had to be commissioned at great expense. Imagine the instructions to the artist:

"Make me something white—it's for a black room, if that helps—and make it like a big shark ghost, okay? Can you do that? But it has to say 'friendly shark ghost' or the chicks will bum. Make it an *abstract* oversize friendly shark ghost. Think you can do that? And can you make it say, 'Whoa, I didn't make the shark a ghost because obviously all the Indian stuff says, I'm the kind of guy who thinks of him as, like, Brother Shark.' Can you do that?"

Apparently so.

I HAVE this horrible vision: it's day one of Alexander Solzhenitsyn's exile in America, and this is where they put him up. *Hope you like it! We just had this room done. There's a desk for writing and everything!* Next morning, they'd find him sleeping in the woodshed.

That wood doesn't go with that wallpaper. Not in this universe. Maybe in some crazy mixed-up universe where quarks are heavy and black holes repel, but not here. Maybe they're like a mismatched cop team in a movie who eventually overcome their differences, learn to trust each other, and realize that their common foe is the puke-green bedspread. But that's a lot to ask of inanimate objects.

Our good friend the Shiny Can has reported for duty as well—this one had a disco ball for a mother, it seems. For an extra-classy touch, an electrified corncob lights up the desktop.

IN GRADE SCHOOL we learned about the planaria: a worm with an arrow-shaped head. Cut it in half, and it grew arrows on both ends. Cut the head in half, and it grew two arrow-shaped heads. Who knew it was also an intestinal parasite unique to interior decorators? A leftover from the '60s pop-art movement, the Planaria Arrow invaded Middle America by the mid-'70s and was instantly adopted as a Bold! Modern! Now! look by people who simply *could not believe* that McGovern lost the election. Notice how the arrow points to the ceiling, drawing your eye to . . . the ceiling. Note how the other arrows point to the corner of the room, drawing your eye to . . . the corner of the room. Yes, let everyone know you're coming up in the world. You've got one of those newfangled corners everyone's talking about.

Nothing points toward Snarky the Clown, who will climb out of the frame after midnight and slaughter the entire family.

THE BOUDOIR of the president of the local chapter of the Guys Who Dress Up As Knights on the Weekend. Come, milady, to a canopy bed fit for a queen! Pillows, fit for a prince! Aggravating scrollwork, fit for a baron! Cheap synthetic carpet that still gives off waves of chemical adhesive aromas, fit for a lab rat! Reflective ceilings, fit for a man anxiously awaiting the results of his syphilis test! Let us drink flagons of wine and talk of noble deeds and crusades and the golden age of body odor! Lo, we shall put on the Genesis records and celebrate chivalrous ideals! Then I will put my William in thine Mary, and— Hey, where you going? I got some good weed! And Chianti! Come back!

no one ever,

ever had sex here. At least not with anyone else.

You can well imagine the fellow who decorated this room—mod vinyl boots. Pete Townsend nose, a lurid boil on his neck, eyes that turned mean with frightening speed. He thought this place would impress women, not realizing that every detail makes his date want to bolt down the stairs. A hard box spring as a make-out bed? Please. A hard cold plastic pillow with hair-oil smears? Gross. And the carpet smells like spilled bong water and magazines that have been left in a damp base-  ment. He puts on "Knights in White Satin" and insists she shut up and listen, and he closes his eyes to show how soulful he is. Well, he does have a van with carpeting in the back. And her parents hate him, which helps.

Something tells her to open her eyes when they're making out. His eyes are wide open. He's watching their reflection in the wallpaper.

Then she looks up at the picture. It's a man's face made of *writhing naked female bodies*. "I really have to leave now," she says—and that's when his eyes narrow: "I thought you were different. *But you're just like the rest.*"

BY ALL MEANS, paint your walls to match the bedspread. You need to learn your lesson. That thing's going to come apart in the wash in a year or so, and nothing you buy will match the meaningless, unappealing sunbaked-Harlequin pattern you've painted on the wall, because by now the design industry is shoving bolts of Day-Glo plaid or paisley-patterned aluminum wallpaper down Americans' throats. "We don't carry that pattern anymore," the clerk will sniff. "You might try a thrift store."

And by all means, get a rug that looks like you had forty Angorans skinned on your command. (There's a naked, embalmed cat on the nightstand as a reminder of this feat.) Remember to turn off the overhead super-hot halogen spot lamp before you sleep—even through closed lids that lamp can burn a hole in your rods and cones, and for the rest of your life it'll always seem as if you're staring directly at the sun. Eventually you'll be stone blind, sitting on a street corner with dark glasses, a can of pencils, and a sign that says, WALLPAPER AND BEDSPREAD ONCE MATCHED. THOUGHT IT MATTERED. PLEASE HELP.

And why the Owl and the Pussycat? Because sometimes in the middle of the night you just bolt up wide-awake and think: *Oh my God, where are my fake-ivory avian and feline statuary?* And you frantically fumble around the nightstand until— *Ahhhhh, there they are.*

I HAD WELTS

like this once after I had eaten some questionable shellfish. It's almost a Zen question: *Where does the bed end and the wall begin, glasshoppah?* The light fixtures seem to fade into the wall, and yes, that's just what you want in a dim, murky room—light fixtures that are indistinguishable from the wall. Come home some night after you've had a few and try to find the lamps—by the time you're done you'll have batted both to the ground and stepped on their shades. Serves you right.

It's a difficult effect to achieve: take several sets of fresh cow lungs, stuff them with explosives, light the fuse, and shut the door.

Excuse me, but who has five lines in their bedroom? In 1972? At least we know how she afforded this groovy room; she pawned the "pound" and "star" keys.

BOB, who had been blind for years, knew there must be *some* reason he frequently dreamed of being smothered by giant canaries, but he could never quite figure out *why*.

SWEET SMOKING JESUS, what was the matter

with these people? It appears that they not only wrapped every door and chair in a blazing plaid, but they also wrapped the mirrors and pictures as well. There are only two possibilities:

A. This is the room in hell reserved for Ralph Lauren.

B. This was a vengeful wife's idea of punishing her stupid, tasteless husband. "Do what you want," he said, "as long as it's plaid. I like plaid. A good red plaid is a solid investment." Okay, she thought: take *this*.

Of course, he loved it.

neuer Buy remnants from nautical-themed glory-hole bars, I say, but that's a matter of personal taste. If one *does* want to take up the designers on this idea, you'll probably have no trouble finding the quilt—the Grandma-American Community turns them out by the millions each year, arthritis be damned—but the headboard is a bit of a different issue. Perhaps there's a network of nineteenth-century cable-spool brokers who can scare one up in a trice, but even if you do get one, you've pretty much assured that your friends will never help you move again. If you live in San Francisco, be glad your friends won't help: imagine standing in another room, packing a box, hearing "uh-oh" outside, and dashing outdoors to watch your headboard bounce down the block at gathering speed before it flies through a plate-glass window and takes out half a dozen shoppers.

Or just imagine a mild earthquake making this thing fall on you while you sleep. Death by cable-spool headboard. The cops couldn't quit laughing as they wrote up the report in telegram style: Get—this—thing-off—me. STOP. Can't—breathe. STOP. Gurghlegglglglggaaaaak. STOP.

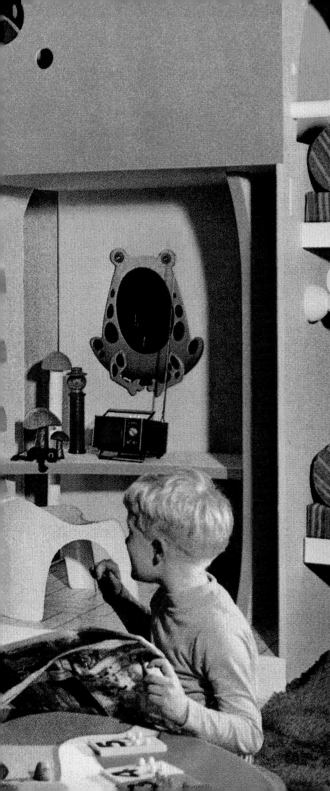

TWINS? *Nein.* This is the supersecret Brazilian Nazi cloning lab, circa 1972. *Hans Eins und Hans Zwei! Iss time für Herr Puffenstuf und a rrration auf Count Von Chocula! Schnell! Schnell!*

It's a great pattern!

Let's use it for the bed! And the frame! And the sofa! And the chair! And the dog! And the driveway! And the lining of our small intestines! And the lawn! And the municipal water tower! And the point where the troposphere meets the ionosphere! Let's persuade NASA to send up satellites that project the pattern on the moon! Let's have it engraved on the insides of our contact lenses! Let's weave it into burial shrouds!

Can't get enough of that pattern!

THE BEDROOM

of Goldfinger's sister,
Pinkfinger. Cue the theme
music:

Pinkfinger!
(da dadada da)
She's the sis—the sis whose
 wretched tastes
This room defaced
(ba-da-da da-dahhh)

Such a stink lingers
(DA DADADA DA!)
From the rug she has in her
 sex-pad lair
That's human hair!

She will talk of the mysteries
 of love
But she only likes things that
 are mauve
Any man will know this date is
 a mistake
Who collects pink frogs, for
 chrissake?

Pinkfinger!

IT'S ALWAYS SAD

when a church goes out of business, but you can pick up some great deals on altar pieces. Particularly if they featured unpopular saints like St. Itych of Vometria or St. Scabbe the Lesser.

More Owl and the Pussycat idolatry, this time from the bric-a-brac shop on the Island of Dr. Moreau: two pieces of the vivisectionist's art, a reddish two-limbed *Feline Erectus* and a melted pink Siamese-twin owl-thing. *Whoooo has bad taste? Whoooo?*

IF YOU FEEL the occasional need to stick your butt in a brown wax hexagon and squirt out some honey, this is the room for you.

no one

likes a headboard that reminds them of a tombstone. But if your dear aunt Mabel sewed you a tombstone, well, you'll have to use it somehow.

Maybe it's a tombstone cozy—one of those things you put over the tombstone to keep it warm. Practical note: To truly unnerve people, use a pillow that looks like a coiled spring. This makes the headboard look as though it's held back by a clasp, and will slam down and crush you with great painful force when released.

kitchen & dining

Few rooms suffered as greatly as the kitchen; few rooms fell this far. Most rooms in a house express the whims of the owners, but kitchens came with their aesthetics pre-installed. You bought a house that had a kitchen with a yellow-tiled wall with a black border and white appliances, you lived with it. That's what everyone had. Oh, they might have had aqua tile with a black border, or seafoam-green tile with a black border, but kitchens had a look, and they'd had one ever since the '30s. Sleek, efficient, modern.

Of course, all that had to go.

You can understand why. The old look was hip when Grandma was twenty-six, whipping up batches of sulfured lard candy for the kids; now it looked tired and old. But too many innocent kitchens were ripped up just when taste had fled the scene. They would have one shot at beauty for the next twenty-five years, and what did they get? Canary-yellow foil wallpaper. Spongy avocado-hued floor tile. Art that made husbands spend decades in silence, wondering if they'll ever be able to ask what the hell that is supposed to *be*.

Since nothing looks older than yesterday's latest thing, these kitchens aged quickly and poorly.

Now nothing says "Grandma" to a thirty-something like a sadly battered harvest-gold toaster in a yard sale.

BY ALL MEANS, group the entire kitchen around a rotating spit. You'll be using that every day. "Kids? Who wants some spit-roasted pancakes with spit-seared muffins? Come on, I've spit-roasted all your Lucky Charms marshmallows just the way you like them."

"Mom, stop saying spit! It's embarrassing!"

The kitchen-as-art-gallery did not gain wide currency any more than the combination garage–baby's room or bathroom-pantry ideas.

It's unlikely that the mistress of the house spends much time here impaling sage-stuffed squabs. To the servants, the mistress is known as She Who Occasionally Enters This Room to Get Ice.

FEELING HEMMED IN by a small room? Well, express your simmering frustrations over your tiny, nonfunctional work spaces by making the walls crawl with claustrophobic patterns. And by all means, commit at least 25 percent of your precious counterspace to a wine rack.

This is the cradle of the '70s "country" style, right here; if only one could go back in time with some oil-soaked rags and a Zippo. Previously, country styles took their cues from the maritime states—a weather vane, some nautical crap, a clay pipe. But here, country has been redefined as this unspeakable quasi–Pennsylvania Dutch dreck that would infect kitchens for twenty years. It speaks to the desire for a more "natural," "authentic," and "itchy" lifestyle that turned its back on the man-made materials and atom-era shapes of postwar design. After all, what did plastic give us? Vietnam and napalm, that's what!

End result for this style's adherents: peasant skirts, granny glasses, hairy legs, green-algae shakes, inability to smile during the Reagan era, and the horrible realization that Tupperware *does* keep weevils out of the flour better than flea-market crocks. No matter how honest the crock may look.

stars and stripes forever.

Really. You couldn't spend more than ten minutes in this room without permanently etching the stars and bars on the inside of your eyeballs.

There's not a Republican in the entire country who'd choose this design. In fact, most Republicans would regard anyone who desecrated the flag in this fashion to be a godless Meathead, and they'd have a point. *All it's lacking is some blue, and I think a nice bruise would do the trick.*

For extra fun, shave your dog and paint him like a zebra.

YOU HaD a FrienD. Your friend had the coolest parents in the world. Your friend's parents were so cool they bought these futury clear-plastic chairs. You begged your own parents: Can we have clear-plastic furniture? No, your mother said. It shows the scratches. It gets cloudy with time, and it's uncomfortable in the summer.

Well, the Johnsons have them, you said, and *they* like them.

The Johnsons also had mirrored wallpaper in the kitchen and white appliances; it was just like the kitchen on *Space: 1999*. Well, not totally. But close.

A few years later, you and your friend realized you could sneak booze out of the Johnsons' liquor cabinet and they'd never miss it. The old man's jacket was usually good for a Winston or two as well. The best part was that they were never around, and they trusted you not to trash the place. Totally cool.

By your senior year you were surprised when the Johnsons divorced. And when your friend was arrested for stealing a car. Moron: he has his own already. What was he trying to prove?

And you wanted plastic chairs, your mom said, raising an eyebrow just like Spock. You'd never seen her do *that* before.

God I HATE my neighbors, part 1

It's possible that someone looked at this window, framed it with thumbs and forefingers, paused to let the tension mount, then said, "Needs spoons." It's more likely that someone saw this in a magazine and decided it was the perfect way to keep those nosy Parkers next door from looking in the window.

Let us now imagine the shoulders of the husband slumping in mute despair as he's handed this picture. *Everything has to balance perfectly, Harry, or there's just no point in doing it.*

Isn't that what you bought that levely thing for? Well, all right, then.

God I HATE my neighbors, part 2

This design suffers from a common delusion that persists to this day: small drawers are useful. They are not. You can call a family meeting, explain the function for each drawer: stamps *here*, coupons *here*, recipes *here*. Hah! In six months each drawer will contain an equal amount of make-up-rate stamps, paper clips, rubber bands, batteries of uncertain charge, pictures of friends' babies you've removed from the fridge but can't bring yourself to throw away, dead pens, leaky pens, screws, a thimble, rusty thumbtacks, small, mysterious pieces of ceramic that broke off God-knows-what, a red bulb from the Christmas lights, a nail clipper, a British coin that some-how showed up in your change one day and whose unexpected appear-ance made you think of the trip to Europe you never took, the exchange

student you had a crush on, and the life you had planned before you married and decided art history wouldn't pay after all. And now here you are in Passaic, making a Metrecal shake so your husband doesn't make cracks about the size of your—

Wait a minute, this is a Canadian coin. Well, you've been there.

Think the neighbors have ever sat in a Montreal café and ordered in French? *Je pense not.*

Think Pernod goes with Metrecal? *Mais oui!*

THE WORST possible chairs for a kitchen. You need chairs you can get in and out of easily, because you'll be up and down a dozen times. These barrel chairs are easy to get into, but unless the cushions are spring-loaded, they're hell to get out of. Maybe there are hooks on the ceilings for ropes, so you can climb out to get the ketchup.

Oh, good: the marble table rests on a plastic pedestal. Near the oven. When that thing goes down someone's going to lose a toe. Or a cat.

Note the proto-microwave, which can cook a potato in a mere hour. Downside: You have to wear a lead vest over genitals and major organs while it's on.

This mysterious object appears to be a statue of Quasimodo in his senior year as a running back for Notre Dame.

THE INVENTOR of Technicolor was sitting right here when they shot him in the head.

A COMFY DINING AREA—if your social circle consists entirely of praying mantises. There's no leg room, no room for plates—unless of course that floral arrangement is the meal, and you suck up the delicious nectar with your thin, chitinous proboscis.

STEP RIGHT UP! Hur-ray hur-ray hur-ray, it's the one-and-only Funhouse Dining Room!

After two glasses of wine, guests walk into the walls when they get up to use the bathroom. People who've been here before run their hands along the wall until they find the door. Once a guest was so desperate he set fire to his napkin just to see how the host ran out of the room.

Bastard doused it with a water goblet.

The den was like the living room, except actual living took place there. Some dens were manly retreats, places where Dad could go with a scotch and a pipe, read Dirk Pitt novels, and break out the *Playboy*s when the kids were down. Some dens were family rooms, also known as rumpus rooms, which sounds better than "Ruckus Hole" or "Random Action Din Cave," but not by much. Most of the dens here bore little resemblance to the average American den. The furniture is new, which contradicts the Den Aesthetic that dens should be in the damp, silverfish-infested basement, with furnishings that used to live upstairs but had been banished to the nether depths when the new living room set came along. Den furniture was relaxed. It didn't care anymore. The pressure was off. The sofas sagged, the tables listed, the bookcase in the corner was something from Grandma's house that Mom painted in a hue she saw in a magazine. Dens were often dank, frowsy dumps, and that's what made them fun. You could spill things. You could maybe scratch something without wondering how you'd cover it up, or blame it on the dog.

These dens and family rooms are just living rooms by another name. Remember: If you can't put your feet up on anything, it's not a den.

yar, matey! It's rum, sodomy, and the sash!

This is "virtual reality," late '60s style. You sit at the desk, eat your cheese sandwich, stare at the shutters while the tape deck plays *Mantovani's Shanties for Lovers*, and pretend the sea heaves beyond those wooden shades.

A glass of milk, a little hornpipe, a night of examining the window treatments for slight historical errors—it doesn't get any better.

A FOURTEEN-YEAR-OLD BOY RECOLLECTS:

Dad thought this was just the coolest room. He called it Bob Johnson's Olde-Fashioned Good-Tyme Family Den and Waterin' Hole, which was okay when he said it around the stupid uncles or his stupid bowling team, but he said it around my friends too, even though I asked him never to call it that. The whole thing was just so phony. Look at the table, and the bench-things—how are you supposed to play a board game, with giant chopsticks? The music stuff was okay but all he listened to was stuff like Ferrante and Teicher, and 101 Strings, and all this crappy stuff with people going *la-la-la* and no guitars. He liked to turn the sound off the TV and make up his own organ accompaniment. We pretty much lost all our friends when everyone came over to watch the Watergate hearings and Dad played ragtime.

GRAVITY SPOT ROOM!

Notice how the laws of physics and perspective seem amazingly warped in this unusual space. Stand in one corner and the room seems to list, to spread, to expand as though defying gravity itself. Even the cans—the all-important hanging crap-crammed cans—hang perfectly parallel to the floor but still seem to lean to the side. It's as if the house is sliding slowly into a big pit already half-filled with 8-tracks, Billy Beer, Erich Segal novels, empty Space Food Stick wrappers, chunky unused Bicentennial notepads, and *TV Guide*s with the special Hudson Brothers cover.

As for that junk in the right-hand corner, it was part of the '70s trend for authentic, back-to-nature items, preferably ones that had been commercially made, machine-dyed, and distributed through a chain store. Whenever you saw this in a house, you were tempted to give it a whack and see a choking cloud of dust, mites, and dead skin cells rise up and coat the furniture.

In fact, if no one ever dusted this room, then that feathery thing might still bear the skin cells of a young impressionable girl who had an aching crush on Bobby Sherman . . . we could clone her—create millions of her, and let them all roam free in a preserve somewhere: Hysteric Park. We have the technology!

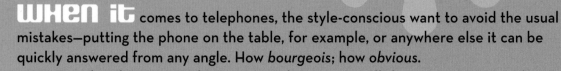

WHEN it comes to telephones, the style-conscious want to avoid the usual mistakes—putting the phone on the table, for example, or anywhere else it can be quickly answered from any angle. How *bourgeois*; how *obvious*.

No. Put the phone in a tight narrow enclosure so small that once you're inside you cannot turn around. Practical tip: put the chair on casters. Not only will this make an inherently unstable chair even more prone to violent upending, but it will make it possible to actually use the booth. It's simple! When the phone rings, pull out the chair, sit down facing the wall, then have someone push you into the booth. Live alone? Don't worry—just use a length of rope to pull yourself into the booth, then propel yourself out by placing your feet flat against the wall and giving yourself a sharp shove.

Since the maneuvering takes some time, make sure all your friends know that you won't answer on the first ten rings.

GOD HELP US,

it's the nightmare arrows again. The attack of the pop-art planaria. Cast your eyes on this Teen Palace—this apotheosis of adolescent design—and weep. For all its busy excitement the reality was stark: three channels of TV and a busted Pong game. Dad was really happy about having his pool room turned into the *phone* room. *Fine,* he said. *Spatter that hippie crap all over a perfectly good room. Just leave me one closet.*

And here's the closet. The Golden Age of Casual Firearm Storage.

NOTHING QUITE SAYS "plaid-jammed alcove" like a plaid-jammed alcove, and this stunning plaid-jammed alcove goes a long way toward proving that time-honored adage. Note how this ancient, abandoned church has been brought up-to-date by wrapping the altar in a buckled tarp. Your guests will fall to their knees—in admiration!

You know, it would be impossible to sit on this sofa without looking as if you disapproved of something. You couldn't cross your legs or lean back; you'd have to sit straight on the edge with your hands on your knees, looking like a Scotsman who'd just been informed of an explosion at the haggis factory.

WHAT'S THE NOVEL?

Rich Man, Poor Man? The Thorn Birds? Everything You Wanted to Know About the Sex Life of a S'more but Were Afraid to Ask? Lord knows how many unsold Gore Vidal books they had to skin to make those cushions. This isn't a chair, it's a Brady-style interrogation chamber. Just add handcuffs. Shackle your kid to the post and let him cook under the cyclopean gaze of the light fixture while you upend his dresser drawers and show him the hash pipes and reefer bags you found. It's a *tough* love seat.

Novel striped love seat

IT'S THE AMAZING new Shelf-O-Shit! Now you have an ideal place to keep your dusty, fragile, indistinguishable crap. Here are some highlights:

A popcorn ball from 1947.

A bittersweet doll head from the Court of Marie-Crapionette.

The amazing new Shelf-O-Shit within a Shelf-O-Shit! And somewhere in this little shelf there's another shelf! And another! And so forth down to the subatomic level where matter merges with the thoughts of God, and that damned spider who nearly killed you when you were fighting over that piece of cake is just a bad memory.

"If You're done with the Syntho-Stim Orb, Logan, I'd like to borrow it; Pleasure Unit 4-A3 is coming over to my domocube after eatshift. Thanks. But wash it off this time first, okay?" This was not a projection of the future. This was the present. This is the vision fobbed off on 1975 Middle America— this horrid *Clockwork Orange* nightmare of glowing orbs and bullying red-oranges, carpets the color of something that comes out of a baby when it has a fever, unstable tables topped with vases that spilled the minute someone bumped them, sofas set so low your knees banged against your ears. It would make an interesting airport bar in Copenhagen, particularly if all the servers wore rubber, but as a home?

HERE'S THE STUMPER. How can the culture that produced the previous room simultaneously produce this kitschy-crawly nightmare? Perhaps that's the lesson to take from all of this—we're not one solid block of citizens with uniform tastes, marching home from work to our sober proletariat cubes. We have the freedom and the money to make over our lives when the whimsy hits. Our houses may look alike from the outside, but behind each door is a riot of mistakes, each appalling in its own unique way.

It takes a mighty nation to endure such bad taste, and we are that nation. But eternal vigilance is necessary. Those who forget the past are doomed to buy it again, thinking that purple suede curtains are "retro." They are not. They are purple suede curtains, and I say to hell with them.

It's up to you. If you worry sometimes that you've lost your way, that an orange bathmat with smiley faces might be cool, or that brown mirrored wallpaper might actually work in the downstairs bathroom, think of Mary Tyler Moore in her black-and-white Dick Van Dyke days: slim as a Salem cigarette in capri pants, the epitome of pre-Nixon, pre-Carter, pre-Waltons, pre-hippie, pre-granola cool.

If you cannot imagine Mary in the room you are about to decorate, don't do it. Your spouse will thank you. Your children will thank you in twenty years. Whoever buys your house after you leave will thank you, inasmuch as they will not curse your bones as they strip off the wallpaper on a muggy July afternoon. Treat your home like a body and remember the ancient physician's motto:

First, do no harm.

Second, do no houndstooth-patterned foil wallpaper.

No, that's not in the physician's creed. But it should be.

about the author

James Lileks is a syndicated political humor columnist for Newhouse News Service and a columnist for the *Star Tribune*. He is the author of *Falling Up the Stairs, Mr. Obvious, Notes of a Nervous Man, Fresh Lies,* and *The Gallery of Regrettable Food.*